WORKBOOK FOR
DAE
TO
LEAD

Brave Work.
Tough Conversations. Whole Hearts

By

Brené Brown

PockeTBooks

Table of Contents

HOW TO USE THE WORKBOOK

This workbook is designed for readers to rise up to the challenges of being a leader. The book "Dare to Lead" is born out of a passion to breed dynamic and savvy leaders. This workbook is to help them explore deeper the means to be a vast leader. This is possible by applying the lessons and following the set action steps provided in this workbook

The lessons therein are simplified enough for readers to understand every action steps devised to aid their desires and aspirations to become purposeful leaders. The checklist prepares the mind of the reader not to miss any lessons or action step in the book. Providing answers to each question helps to get a full appraisal of the message communicated in this book.

Leading is experiential. Remember to enjoy the experience and have fun throughout the workbook

INTRODUCTION

The book *Dare To Lead* by Brown, Brene, is a book designed for everyone, right from the person who is aspiring to be a leader, already a leader, having troubles with leading, running away from leadership or unable to maintain leadership. It enables readers to see how a leader can face and surmount challenges while enjoying the allure of being a leader. It brings to the fore the experience of Brene and how she has been able to face and lead so many people at different times, what she has been able to accomplish, her set regimen before each time she faces her team.

This is not your average Questions and Answer workbook. It is written to aid your ability to grasp exactly what the major book is about. It is designed to aid your decision-making process. If all guidelines, checklists, to-do lists and action steps in this workbook are followed to the max, it will help you live above mediocrity and indent a permanent lifestyle of excellence to enhance your journey to success and mental courage

Remember, the barriers and obstacles to daring leadership are real and sometimes fierce. However, they do not have the power to stop us from being brave.

INTRODUCTION: BRAVE LEADERS AND COURAGE CULTURES

There is a great need for leaders to be groomed everywhere. From corporations, non-profits, public and private sector organizations to government, activist groups, schools, and faith communities. The need for leaders to arise is now specifically urgent and we are all called to be leaders at one point in our lives or another.

Points to be noted

- A leader must not have selfish goals as it will breed a know-it-all mentality.
- The first lesson every leader must learn is that studying about leadership is easier than leading.
- Importance should be placed on emotional pulls and bandwidth as they can affect output.
- The first leading starts from the home. A great leader is one who is able to manage the internal pressures from the home, as in family and external pressure as in managing external factors.
- One who can stay calm under emotionally challenging situations has the makings of a great leader.
- A leader is one who can take responsibility for finding potentials in people and process, and who has the courage to develop that potential.
- A courageous leader is one who has a knack for honest and productive feedback, one is committed to taking risks and pushing forward without making time for unproductive conversations. He/She identifies problem real fast and makes time to critically analyze exactly how to solve them.

QUESTIONS

1. What skills do you need to be called a brave leader?

_____
_____
_____
_____
_____
_____
_____
_____

2. Should a brave leader accept the blame for every decision gone bad?

_____
_____
_____
_____
_____
_____
_____
_____

3. How can a leader make a team of courageous leaders from followers?

_____
_____
_____
_____
_____
_____
_____
_____

THE HEART OF DARING LEADERSHIP

Courage and fear are like two emotional bottles that we hold at the same time. The one we drink from is the one our minds actually feed us. The exact emotional skill-set we need is not far from us. Struggling with the mind to give it the right nudge makes us feel off and respond to fear when what we actually need is courage.

Lessons to be noted

- Vulnerability to courage and fear brings us to our rumble time. That time when we have the deepest conversation with ourselves. To bring courage and daily practice that can support us during the rumble. A daring leader must have the foundational skill of courage building.
- The thoughts of a leader are reflected on the team he/she leads
- Courage is not an inherited trait. The true obstacle to brave leadership is the response a leader gives to fear. Do you respond in fear or courage?
- A brave leader must create an environment which breeds positivity and strength every time. The environment should be one where everyone can speak, be heard and noticed.
- A brave leader must have a thorough and deep connection to the ones they lead. This will imprint on their followers that they have a leader who keeps up with their schedules and plans.
- Followers will only give in good ideas when they are made to feel comfortable and championed in the right cause. Making them feel important will increase their production level
- Enough space without suffocation births a courageous leader and a courageous team.

QUESTIONS

1. Why do you find it so hard to give your team space to chip in their ideas?

Child safty will f suer, doeing it right

2. What skills are you expecting from your team before they are ready to pipe in their creatives?

all ideas, listen.

3. As a leader, which member of your team can you allow to lead? What are the possible reasons?

assist Director
Most Knowledge

4. What are the qualities of your best team member?

good listner
Calm level head

5. In your view, what type of leader are you?

so-so

PART ONE: RUMBLING AND VULNERABILITY

COURAGE IS CONTAGIOUS

SECTION ONE: THE MOMENT AND THE MYTHS

Vulnerability is the emotion that is unleashed when we feel uncertain and unsure moments. It is like the toxin that either fuels our creatives or makes our fear come to the fore. There is a great need for a leader to have a strong team plus a big armor that will stop us from feeling hurt from the things we hear when we are vulnerable. Vulnerability is positive and negative. How we use our vulnerabilities is what matters. We do not need to shut ourselves off from being vulnerable. To love is to be vulnerable in itself.

LESSONS TO BE NOTED

- Feedback is important. Every leader needs to know the opinion of people. However, the opinions a leader prioritize is what matters.
- Every cheap-set feedback should not be put to reckoning. Wasting energy on them is like spending essential time meant for useful things to solve useless criticism which might bring shame and reduce productivity. A daring leader should not be held back by criticisms.
- The people in your team should be those who can stick for you in your absence. Those that can chip in their ideas without being scared. Those who can make you know the next point of action in every vulnerability
- Vulnerability is not weakness. Courage only comes when

vulnerability sets in. The mother lifting a car off her child, the soldier taking on five rebels at a time are all borne out of their vulnerabilities.

- You need to understand vulnerability. Pretending that you are not vulnerable is allowing the fear of being vulnerability hold you down.
- A team needs players. Vulnerability makes you feel like you don't need anyone but the truth is life runs on connections and these connections are only found when there is a team.
- Managing and controlling your vulnerabilities need you to embrace the vulnerabilities first. Getting to understand the frustrations, the uncertainty, the risks, the downs, and all the emotions makes the vulnerability easier to manage and win.
- Trusting your team does not make you vulnerable. You only need to choose a team of people who will have your back and their loyalty. Vulnerability is not the first step for betrayal.
- We need to be trusted to be vulnerable and we need to be vulnerable to win trust. In other words, vulnerability brings up trust. This is how courageous leaders are made.
- Building trust takes a gradual, intuitive and slow-paced process that happens over time. Trust and vulnerability is a risk. For one to trust means courage. For one to be vulnerable to win trust, there must be courage.
- A courageous and daring leader must share with their followers their mindsets and how they feel. Building bonds among team players means that there must be discussions on fears and emotional displacements.
- Growing leaders comes from bonding with followers. Rumbling comes from vulnerability. A daring leader must understand that followers have all reasons to have an emotional attachment to their leader.
- Disclosure during vulnerability brings feedback among team members. It builds confidence as they know what is in the mind of everyone in the team.
- Holding to emotional bottlenecks can cause psychological grips on the team as there may be friction among team

members. There must be honesty. A daring leader living honestly with the team increases the courage growth ratio in the team.

- Only a fake leader gives a chance to ask questions without a guaranteed psychological safety to do it or not stopping for others to talk during a conversation. That is a fake vulnerability.
- Everything should not be called vulnerability just because they look like vulnerability. Fake vulnerability is when people are manipulated to become vulnerable. Vulnerability is not a personal market tool.
- Setting boundaries is great but creating a seamless environment where everyone can share and unburden creates a strong working force and less vulnerable to fear.
- A daring leader must allow everyone to participate. Every one must have a defined role. It will increase productivity and make everyone ready to chip-in their ideas
- To feel is to be vulnerable. Believing that vulnerability is a weakness is believing that feelings are the same thing as weaknesses.
- An unshakable truth every daring leader should know is that vulnerability is the cornerstone of courage. Without vulnerability, there will be no creativity. In other words, vulnerability is the foundation of every known invention.
- Being vulnerable brings adaptability, a skill every courageous leader must have. Vulnerability hinges on feelings.
- Vulnerability is where every purpose and creativity is found

QUESTIONS

1. How do I act when I feel vulnerable?

_____

_____

_____

_____
_____
_____
_____
_____

2. In what situations has my vulnerability brought me inventions and ideas?

_____
_____
_____
_____
_____
_____
_____
_____

3. What type of talk would I give my team when we are faced with a challenge that is tasking for all of us?

_____
_____
_____
_____
_____
_____
_____
_____
_____
_____

4. What qualities are you expecting from your team to trust them?

_____
_____
_____
_____

_____

_____

_____

_____

_____

_____

_____

5. Can I tell my team members my vulnerabilities?

_____

_____

_____

_____

6. What vulnerabilities do you have?

_____

_____

_____

_____

_____

_____

_____

_____

_____

7. What are the roles of each team member?

_____

_____

_____

_____

_____

_____

SECTION TWO: THE CALL TO COURAGE

Time is an important dogma a leader must have in their mind. Procrastination is one of the things a courageous leader must never entertain. That events or happenings are months away doesn't mean the needed things to be done will happen perchance. Creating timelines is an easy task for anyone. Anyone can have a set target of what will happen in a matter of weeks or months or years in the mind. It might be as well written down but taking action to make sure the set goals or set plan for that time is accomplished is where the real work is. Accurate and proper timing is one important principle a daring leader must follow. Having all day doesn't mean waiting all day to do what is to be done.

LESSONS TO BE NOTED

- Of all things, a courageous leader must recognize his/her ability to keep or not keep up with time. It takes someone courageous to do that.
- A daring leader must have a team that will hold him responsible for any flaw or delay in service delivery
- The first person accountable in the team is always the leader. A leader should not be afraid of being accountable for his/her failures. Failure to be accountable is giving the whole team an initiative to become irresponsible.
- Give responsibilities according to the capability of each team member.
- Each member of a team has certain strengths, weaknesses, and skillsets. Hence, you should give responsibilities based on what you observe that the team member can do. It will increase productivity when they are made to do what they are good at.

- Estimating timing is better committed to one who is good with the kinetics of keeping to time. Timing needs one who is precise, profound, and intentional.
- Feeding people half-truths to make them feel better is clearly unkind. It is better to be clear with a colleague, team member about their roles or responsibilities. It makes it easier for them to know when they are patronized or deserve the commendation
- It is bad to talk about team members behind them. It is not a mark of a courageous leader. It increases distrust and brings in in too much frustration with team members as their faults are magnified while their achievements are less celebrated
- Giving team members time to rumble on what to do or what they have done is not weakness. It is strength to allow people to get their priorities straight. People need the short breaks or thinking times to reorganize their wit and increase productivity. It is to the increase in productivity of the team when members are granted few days to regain strength, it makes them sharper.
- It is not weakness to know every team member's qualities. A leader must be able to know when/where a team member will be a hitch and when/where they will be the grease to the team's efforts
- Creating an atmosphere of ease makes it less tedious for each member to display new skills they acquired. Their feeling of anger, less-confidence will only reduce their productivity levels and this would cause a clog to the team.
- A courageous leader should know his qualities as well. Being a leader is not about being a jack of all trades, master of none. It is no shame or weakness for a leader to admit to not having a needed quality or skill in the team.
- A courageous leader is one who has mastered the elements of key learning. Each member will become honest and open to communication when the leader is displaying the same enthusiasm to learn just as he is offering to teach the members.
- Fear makes us increase our armor of distrust for team

members. There will be no honesty. Team members become competitors instead of partners. The atmosphere becomes uncomfortable and they are made to be the fall option for every blame.

- Leaders do not have to know all before they are deemed courageous or daring. They can do so little. It is how truthful and skilled they are with their little that makes them the daring leaders they are.
- Sharing experiences and giving pep-talks is not a waste of time. It is a way to increase bonding and show that a leader is committed to improving the qualities and productivity of the team members
- Learning to control fear is one way to stop procrastination. Offloading emotions on team members makes the relationship toxic. Replacing unproductive members is good but how great is replacing team members that reduced productivity and creatives because they are unsure of what response will be to their daring initiative?
- Daring leaders seek to improve themselves every day just as they try to improve their team members and followers.
- There should be team meetings where every attendee is giving time to pipe-in their thoughts. It allows everyone to feel like a part of the decision process and increase their mental strength.
- The easiest and most difficult skill a daring leader would need to have is the ability to apologize to team members. As much as getting credit for decisions is great, it is also great that leaders are ready to apologize when decisions taken doesn't bring in the expected results. It shows a leader who is courageous enough to know when they fail. It is no weakness, it is a great strength.
- Leaving team members for a long time without involving them will bring loneliness which can make them vulnerable
- The world is witnessing different paradigm in every shift and sector. It is now an accepted that humanness is not a weakness when displayed but a bond if when worked on can increase the productivity of the team and what values they should have and

represent
- A courageous leader is accessible to every team member it makes it easier for each member to come with their bunch of ideas and information. It also makes the leader look trustworthy to them.
- Building trust is opening up to vulnerability. It makes leaders see the capabilities and honesty of every team members.
- Leaders that connect with their members always have team members who are daring and ready to stand for the ethos of what they have struggled to achieve over the years than leaders who are closed and manual.
- Granting team members time to retrain shows that the leader wants improvement for them. Having team members learn other skills show that the leader wants growth and interdependence of team members.
- Sharing experiences of failures is not a sign of weakness. Telling stories of past achievement is not a sign of strength either. Study the mood of your team to give the right stories they will be invested in. Daring leaders are innovative and non-conformist; they improvise.
- Giving opportunities for members to ask questions after presentations show them the value of confidence and related growth. Not making time to hear feedback makes a team meeting look like an information pitching exercise. It will be monolithic and monotonous. At the end, team members will not be invested in to the meetings

QUESTIONS

1. What do I do when my team members feel lonely?

_____
_____
_____
_____

_____

_____

_____

_____

_____

_____

2. What is my part in building confident team members?

_____

_____

_____

_____

_____

_____

3. How willing am I to allow team members to give their opinions
and ideas?

_____

_____

_____

_____

_____

_____

4. If I were to be a team member, would I love to have me as the
team leader?

_____

_____

_____

_____

_____

_____

5. What would I tell a team member who's tired but willing to

continue with duties?

_____

_____

_____

_____

_____

_____

_____

6.In your definition, what is humanness?

_____

_____

_____

_____

_____

_____

7. Rating my experience, what has been the standpoint of team meetings that I enjoy?

_____

_____

_____

_____

_____

_____

8. What qualities are expected of team members if they are allowed to join decision making?

_____

_____

_____

_____

_____

_____

_____

9. What words will I use when I am to apologize to the team for a wrong or miscalculated decision?

_____

_____

_____

_____

_____

_____

_____

_____

_____

_____

10. How can I increase the performance of lonely members?

_____

_____

_____

_____

_____

_____

_____

SECTION THREE: THE ARMORY

The world as it is now is dictated by the enormousness of not just the muscles, but the brain. The brain is the added beauty on which every decision is hinged. It is erroneous to think that leading is all about having a big body or huge stockpile of brains. Amazingly, the world is witnessing a paradigm shift from machine-like workers to emotional, spirited, committed, passionate workers who are endeared to what they do. It is rewarding to help employees to have a passion for what they do. Through this, they will be intentionally productive in everything they do. Fighting vulnerabilities is like entering into a self-protect mode, one which won't allow for forward-thinking, critical analysis, progressive process and creative ideas

LESSONS TO BE NOTED

- Team members who are passionate and wholehearted are interestingly hard to find. It is like trying to find a needle in a haystack, there will be lots of injuries and bruises until the needle is seen. Wholehearted teammates are built.
- To be wholehearted means to be ready for integration with the team. Releasing the armor of fear and historical references gives a chance for better familiarity with each team member which will increase productivity and trusting the leader.
- Been emotional is not a weakness. It is a sign of the humanity in us and how we react to happenings. A daring leader would allow team members to understand the place of their emotions and how it impacts on their productivity
- There is no way anyone who is not committed to a work can be productive. Severing the heart or becoming emotionless just for the sake of the team is the beginning of the downfall of the team. Seeing vulnerabilities as liabilities is tantamount to building individual team member out of unity.
- Having hard conversations with the team is one of the ways to

gauge the wholeheartedness of each member.

- Although we act like it is not happening, the truth is emotions still control our thoughts and influence our decisions. When the heart is open and free, the right connection to emotions will happen. It will ease the creativity and impart bright ideas.
- Each team member needs to be shown how valuable they are to the success of the team. Ego is the beginning of demolishing the good imparts a great team would have had.
- The reason leaders do not want to have conversations with their team members is because they are afraid of opening their heart to the members to understand exactly what they are thinking.
- The ego is a just a killing driving force which shut out those who should be paying attention to hearing us from the heart. Ego is an eager and willing conspirator that locks away the heart
- A daring leader must improve his speech-making skills. It is the most important way to gain access to the heart of the team.
- Perfectionism is not the apogee of excellence, self-improvement or forward focus. It is born out of selfishness and it is a function of shame. It makes one set up a system of looking for those who would take the fall for any mistake of the team
- Perfectionism is a self-destructive and addictive belief system based o the principles of seeking for a chain result of doing things perfectly to minimize the guilt of blame, judgment and shame.
- As important as being perfect is, it creates a system of troubleshooting and distrust among team members as there will always be the one to take the fall for the whole of the team. It imparts to the team that someone is not good enough or their input was the causation of the extant result the team is having.
- Daring leaders are great talkers.
- Perfectionism can only be achieved in a brave and trusting team, not one where everyone feels harangued and susceptible

to be attacked when the need arises for it.

- In a brave team, it is okay to discuss the tenets of perfectionism. This is because the team itself is already working on the tenets of delivering perfection and just need little work for their ideas to work.
- It is great for a team to celebrate victories as it gives them enough grounds to prepare for the next challenge. Refusing to celebrate because of the next challenge is like holding down on the huge drive celebration brings.
- Naturally, joy celebration brings the next line of action and increases doubt. It is the feeling of perfection to not allow team members or employees to not celebrate present victories because there is another level or much to be done. A daring leader should know how to manage the team members or employees while celebrating so that they don't take the foot off the gas and don't lose the essence of why they celebrate.
- Having a record of achievements and success is a great step to increasing happiness of team members. It makes them aware of the battles they have won, the milestones they have achieved, the records they have set. A daring leader uses that as a legal ground to challenge the team, that is gratitude and action.
- Gratitude is life. It is allowing the whole team to see how vulnerable they once were and how they were able to piece things together to record their present victories. It is called the pleasure of accomplishment. It is needless to say that a courageous leader must be an orator as words have a way of reaching the heart than some actions do.
- Giving teammates slogans or keywords to hold on to when there are difficulties is not a sign of a weak or unfocused leader. Instead, it is the duty of a leader to seek ways that will improve the productivity of the team.
- Words like "Easy does it" "take it slowly" "one step at a time" "Slow and steady" "wherever you go, there you are", might look like a child's lullaby but when hammered on in the ears of the team, it becomes the bedrock of how they face their

challenges and win battles.

- One of the biggest ways to get wholeheartedness from team members is to see when the team is struggling and grant them leave. It is called renewing the spirit. Give team holidays, one which team members go together to reload.
- Giving team members a sense of belonging increases how trusting and wholehearted they would turn out to be.
- To have integration and cohesion in the team, the team must have the same mentality. In other words, the team's growth must be in unison, not individualistic team growth. Growing individually will only increase the team's distrust of each member, and at the end, everyone will only be seeking to outdo each other
- Team meetings should allow everyone to talk, offer suggestions, and contribute. This singular act stimulates creativity and increases innovation. Daring leaders are not afraid to bring everyone to see what is happening in the team or company as this will reduce or eradicate criticism from the cheapest places
- Giving team members the sense of belonging will reduce team members competing to outdo each other. Give team commendations openly not in your mind. Give personal eulogies secretly. The team is valuable, each team member is valued.
- Daring leaders should not at any time, exaggerate the importance of an individual over the cohesion of the team. It gives each team members ideas to start pushing to get the same commendation. While that is good for productivity, it is bad for the values and ethos of the team.
- Daring leaders explain strategies to the team and share smaller tasks to everyone. Explaining strategies gives the team the strength of decision making. Sharing smaller tasks is tied to achieving larger goals and purpose. In the end, every member will be happy they contributed their little quota to the big result.
- Only compelling leaders learn how to leverage fear and make

it a weapon that work it at their advantage. Daring leaders are not autocrats who bring people's fears to the fore as an enhancement for them to work faster.

- Daring leaders use a system of checklists that sort out employees or team's fears. Using the TASC (Task Accountability, Success, Checklist) approach is so far, a great way to help team members. Each member is tasked according to their capability. The task makes them accountable as they must give results. The success is recognized. And the checklist of what has been done is noted

- During times of scarcity, it is pertinent to embrace the uncertainty. The team needs to share strengths with each other, this is only done when each member open up. The leader needs to check every claim that is made during this period as a lot of possibilities that can make the team implode can be shared.

- Inclusivity of everyone in the team is non-negotiable. Creating a culture of belonging is the beginning of bonding. Understanding the diversity in culture, language or belief among the members makes the team respect the leader.

- Lifting the morale of the team is as important as lifting the mood of the leader. Giving the team reward while neglecting the efforts of the leader is one way to become not just a daring leader but an endeared leader. Prioritizing the mood of the team makes the team feel honored and increase productivity.

- Using the armor of hurt to lead a team will make the leader shift blames to the team

- Stopping to breathe, or asking for leave of absence, or taking a few days off is not a bad idea for the leader. It shows how much you trust the team when you leave affairs in their hands for some time

- Having conversations from the heart is not a bad trait. It shows the passion of the leader and how much he's invested in to winning together with the team. A daring leader considers the team before making decisions.

- Leadership means feeling the pains, joys, passion,

commitment, and emotional of the ones that are led. A reasonable amount of time is therefore needed to be invested to attending to team members; their fears and strength.

QUESTIONS

1. What reaction would I give when team members ask me an uncomfortable question?

_____
_____
_____
_____
_____
_____
_____
_____

2. What are the words needed to create connections with team members?

_____
_____
_____
_____
_____
_____
_____
_____

3. How do I reach out to team members who become tired and wants to quit?

_____
_____
_____
_____
_____
_____

_____
_____

4. What style of leadership have I been using? Autocratic, compelling, persuasive or courageous?

_____
_____

5. How do I make team members realize their roles and increase their productivity?

_____
_____
_____
_____
_____
_____
_____
_____

6. What do I do when team members get anxious?

_____
_____
_____
_____
_____
_____
_____

7. Which is important? Celebrating team's progress or team member's efficiency?

_____
_____
_____
_____

_____
_____
_____

8. Which of these words is suitable for the team? Power to, Power within, Power with?

_____
_____
_____
_____
_____
_____
_____
_____

9. Which is better? Thinking for the team or thinking with the team?

_____
_____
_____
_____
_____
_____
_____
_____

10. What is my part in building the confidence of my team to share suggestions with me without fear or trepidation?

_____
_____
_____
_____
_____
_____
_____
_____

SECTION FOUR: SHAME AND EMPATHY

Shame is the *'never good enough'* emotion. It makes a leader not ready to own up to responsibilities or own up to faults or take the blame for any fault. Instead, it brings a certain vulnerability that leads to feelings of being unworthy, never enough, blow to self-worth and then the fear of what will happen if we own up to this numbing rumble.

It increases anxiety levels and makes one feel exceptionally unreliable as we do not want to agree with the things we need to do or ought to do. We struggle emotionally to act like we are in charge but deep down, we know it won't kill to admit to struggling and needing help. The admittance is the problem because compelling leaders believe that this makes them weak. So, they carry on with the aura of inadequacies, believing that they are the ones who carry the team and should not admit to struggling. Admittance will lead to finding help within the team but so far, this is the place where the real courageous leaders are separated from any other type of leaders.

Having empathy is one of the attitudes that endear team members to leaders. An empathetic leader is always seen as strong no matter the inadequacies and flaws such a leader has.

LESSONS TO BE NOTED

- The first step to fighting vulnerability is agreeing that we need help. Sadly, most leaders find that difficult to do. They believe they are high and above normal mood changes and swings.
- Build up a team that will know when to press the right panic button. Everyone has the one who calms them. Having your team know the right person to ask to speak to you shows that you have bonded with them so well.

- The first display of mood swing is combative actions, frustrated talks, tired and jaded looks. Stress is not limited to team members alone. A leader is also susceptible to tiredness.
- Being sick is not lazy. The body has a way it armors up when it notices that it is not getting enough rest. Sometimes, the illness we have just needs a little bedtime.
- There are many things a leader needs to learn, relearn and unlearn. It won't kill to know few things from team members. It is humbling and rewarding to learn from them.
- Plans proposed can be disposed by actions greater than our powers. Acts of God can cancel set actions. Be empathetic and sympathize with team members. It makes them know how much you care about them
- Shame is universal. The ones who can't or won't experience shame are the ones who lack the capacity for empathy and human connection.
- No one wants to talk about shame because it makes us feel odd. Naturally, no one wants to admit to their flaws and inadequacies or struggles
- We all have the feeling of being unworthy of so many good things we get. Love, happiness, connection, even joy.
- Shame makes people retreat in to their old selves. Team members who display attitudes of sudden silence, lack of assurance, unbelief are having the guilt of shame in their heart.
- Shame makes people have bad intuitions even when great and good things happen to them. Shame is when team members cannot identify with their teammates in public or share things with each other. Bonding will naturally die and the essence of having a team is defeated.
- The best way to solve and sort shame is to differentiate between guilt and shame. Guilt brings shame. Guilt is never the result of shame.
- If shame is not noticed on time, it can lead to destructive behavior, hurtful hates, distasteful competitions with another team, and self-aggrandizing behavior.
- Empathy is the opposite of shame. It is the part that sees beyond

the letdowns that shame has earmarked. It is a powerful and adaptive emotion for daring leaders.

- Humiliation is confused with shame. A team member's understanding of the two explains what reaction he will give. Leaders need to pinpoint words that won't humiliate team members in public. It takes away their perfect happy aura and replaces it with shame and guilt

- Constant humiliation makes for a miserable and toxic work environment. If it continues without check, it will lead to shame.

- There are signals a leader must not show. These signals make team members form ideas which will lead to push for individualistic responsibilities. A leader should not reveal a favorite team member. Doing so will cause other members to start displaying negative attitudes

- A daring leader should not be found bullying others, criticizing subordinates in front of colleagues, delivering public reprimands or setting up reward system that is to intentionally shame or humiliate employees or team members

- Criticizing people in front of others can damage their self-worth and value. Their shame value is increased and their creativity becomes scarred. It reduces how much team members are willing to have a confrontation with the leader.

- Easing or firing people, re-assigning their roles is one of the difficult decisions a leader will take. However, it should not be done in the public to shame them. Making them keep their dignity gives them enough respect to leave with their heads held high.

- Making people feel ashamed is like killing the human in you. Give consideration to how the person will be impacted by your words, gestures, actions and sequence.

- Delivering or giving or sharing bad news should not be done to shame the receiver. Kindness is needed. Give enough respect and be generous. In some situations, it is better to allow the person to resign than be fired.

- Giving them the choice of selecting how they would like their colleagues to know gives them more emotional boost and confidence. No matter what team members do, allowing them to keep their dignity shows how courageous and daring you are

- There is no one that is shame resistant. But shame resistance is teachable. It is the ability to come out on the other side of the shameful experience with more courage, strength and compassion. The antidote to shame is EMPATHY
- Empathy is agreeing with the person that what they feel is real and that we understand. It is like telling them what is happening to them is normal, a trait which every normal human should have. You have to find the soft spot to start from or they won't agree to the shame.
- Empathy is not reducing the pain. It is rather a chain of actions that is to reflect the truth of how the feeling is and making them realize the importance of their own efforts. A daring leader should know the exact way to react to team members setbacks and failure.
- In empathy, you have to understand that the opinion and perspectives of others will be different from ours, therefore you need to allow others to share their own views.
- A courageous leader must stamp out judging team members. Straight-forward judging will reduce how empathetic we can get. It will impart on the words we use and the actions we take.
- Empathy is seeing the world from the perspective of other parties but it gives room for telling how we see what we see. It won't kill to not understand how they feel but try to make efforts to.
- Empathy is emotional literacy. Understanding this will make it easier to know what emotions each team member is communicating and the best way to respond
- Pain is not possible to be ignored and there is no certainty of emotions. Empathy is, therefore, more about connection and the ability to reroute words. Paying attention to people make them admit to whatever shame they are facing.
- Sympathy is not empathy. Showing empathy is feeling the exact emotions they are feeling with them. Been sympathetic is feeling pity for their plight, something most people would never

like

● Connecting with people need more than words. It needs the right actions, the right feel, the right questions and the right motivation.

QUESTIONS

1. How do you manage team members who do not own up to being ashamed?

_____

_____

_____

_____

_____

_____

_____

_____

2. What feeling of shame have you felt as a team leader?

_____

_____

_____

_____

_____

_____

_____

_____

3.   What is my team mission, purpose and values?

_____

_____

_____

_____

_____

_____
_____
_____

4. How committed am I to tackling problems that threaten our mission, vision and values?

_____

_____

5. How can I maker the team connect with intentions that drive my thoughts, feelings and actions?

_____

_____

SECTION FIVE: CURIOSITY AND GROUNDED CONFIDENCE

Confidence is a key emotional factor to be built by members of a team. Having grounded confidence is a key process which requires learning and unlearning, practicing and failing, and surviving a few misses. Curiosity is the beginning of building a courageous team. To have a curious team is to have a team which is committed to solving problems and issues that arise at each turn.

LESSONS TO BE NOTED

- There are some important skills and emotions which are needed to be drilled into the team before the duty starts.
- Developing a disciplined practice of rumbling with vulnerability gives the leader the strength and emotional stamina to dare greatly.
- In tough conversations, hard meetings and emotionally charged decision making, leaders need the grounded confidence to stay tethered to their values rather than react emotionally.
- Being curious makes you open to improvements, new openings, and meeting challenges.
- Easy learning doesn't build strong skills. Make the team understand that having easy learning facilities and schemes does not bring lasting learning. Effective learning needs to be effortful. A daring leader needs to increase a team's capability and capacity through a series of tasking learning that heightens their curiosity for improvement.
- Curiosity brings with it creativity, intelligence, improved learning, memory increase and problem-solving capacities. The changes everybody feels when they are curious makes them better learners and retain more information as the capacity of the brain is enhanced.
- People are afraid to be curious because they are scared to have

hard conversations about how to solve the problem we are facing and how to go about it.

- To lead effectively, we are responsible for respecting and leveraging the different views and staying curious about how they can often conflict.
- Giving people tit-bits on reasons to heighten their curiosity will only help the team to become more productive and improve.
- Being curious makes the leader and team self-aware of what they never thought they can do.
- A daring leader should be intentional about building enough trust and connection to talk about equity issues; to commit to helping those who need to silently acquire the skills and grounded confidence to participate in tough and hard conversations
- A courageous leader should be committed to investing in building high-performing, connected teams by using strength-based and work-personally assessments and developed structured protocols for hard conversations, including progress checks.

QUESTIONS

1. What facilities and provisions have I made for the improvement of my team?

_____
_____
_____
_____
_____
_____
_____
_____

2. What strategy is best adopted to improve my team and I?

_____

_____

_____

_____

_____

_____

_____

_____

3. Which of my team members displays the greatest curiosity skills?

_____

_____

_____

_____

_____

_____

_____

4. How constant should I make time to check my personal life and development?

_____

_____

_____

_____

_____

_____

_____

5. What are those things that has made my team produce beyond expectations, in the past?

_____

_____

_____

_____

PART TWO: LIVING INTO OUR VALUES

Daring leaders are the ones who see their challenges and issues but are not daunted. They are dauntless and do not respond to distractions. The value of a daring leader is one who always remembers the reason they are where they are, particularly during the dark and hard times. Being brave is to be daring. There are those moments that question our very qualities of being a leader, remembering to not let them hijack our thoughts but choosing to stay above water due to the value we have created is living into our values

LESSONS TO BE NOTED

- A daring leader sets priorities straight. The first step of living into our values is defining the most important qualities and skills to us.
- The team's focus, the leader's mindset should not be changed based on recent or present happenings. There is always a set value or standard which the team has attained and must be sustained.
- The values of the team, i.e the achievements and pedestal of the team should be clear in the minds of every team member.
- The team, no matter how pressed or uneasy, should always strive to pick what is right over what is easy. That is sustaining value.
- Making the team valuable is not as important as making it a behavior of each team member that they are valuable. That is translating values from ideals to behavior
- The team is equally important when thinking of sustaining the values. Empathy and self-compassion are two important value skills that daring leaders have to choose from. As a matter of fact, team leaders do not shy away from hard decisions and things
- The team needs to stay aligned to the values even when giving

and receiving feedback. Listening skills, readiness to give feedback, tackling issues together, acknowledgment of the word 'us', putting team strengths into consideration resolving challenges together are all ways to build and grow team values together

- Sharing values is a massive trust and connection builder for teams. A leader should be proud of the team he leads.
- Set the right values and key values for the team to learn, know and follow.
- If we want to be value-driven, we have to operationalize our values into behaviors and skills that are teachable and observable

QUESTIONS

1. What are my professional and personal values?

_____
_____
_____
_____
_____
_____
_____

2. Which of the team members know the value of the team and makes effort to live them?

_____
_____
_____
_____
_____
_____

3. What are the early warning indicators that the team is living outside the values?

_____

_____

_____

_____

_____

_____

4. How far have I gone to understand each team member's personal value?

_____

_____

_____

_____

_____

5. On a scale of 1- 10, how would I rate my team member's understanding of the core principles and values of the team?

_____

_____

PART THREE: BRAVING TRUST

When you trust someone, you are allowing yourself to be vulnerable to a person's actions. Trust begets integrity. And no matter how great our integrity value is, there will always be challenges to our trusts. The slightest inkling that someone is questioning our trustworthiness doesn't mean we should set total vulnerability lock-down in motion.

LESSONS TO BE NOTED

- Once we are in lock-down, we can not hear anything that is being said because we become hijacked. Our emotional system switch to survival mode and everything goes on shut down
- Trust is a must have. However, many leaders try to avoid discussions about trust because there is no exactness from those who are having the discussion with them. The more exact we are, the more likely it is that people can hear us.
- To build trust among members, a leader can devise a conversation guide or discourse that seeks to walk members through conversations from a place of curiosity, learning and most importantly, trust building.
- Setting talk boundaries creates reliable discussions and makes team members accountable which would lead to an increase in trust building.
- Integrity is choosing courage over comfort; it is choosing what is right over what is fun, or easy; and it is practicing your values, not just professing them.
- Every man has the element of seeking to bring out the prick in others. The desire to judge is strong in most team members.
- Asking for help is not a betrayal of trust among team members. Instead, it leads to an increase in capacity building and stretching capacity.
- A daring leader is always a better listener and a better speaker. A leader should have a team that can be trusted and brave

enough to deal with the stuff that is always easier to avoid.

- The best way to live is to choose what is right over what is easy. It makes the team trust the value system in place.
- There are specific work styles and culture that suits each team. Leaders should, therefore, encourage their team to work together to develop one or two observable behaviors.
- The foundation of trust with others is based on our ability to trust ourselves. Unfortunately, self-trust is one of the first casualties when we fail, fall or have disappointments
- There are key seven elements to build self-trust; bravery, reliability, accountability, vault, integrity, non-judgment, generosity. Being in control of this is the first way to have a happy team that trust their value and work no matter the outcome.

QUESTIONS

1. What boundaries need to be in place for me to be seen as integrity?

_____

_____

_____

_____

_____

2. How can I be generous with my assumptions about the intentions, words and actions of others?

_____

_____

_____

_____

_____

_____

3. What are those habits I develop when I don't like the outcome of

my team's effort?

_____

_____

_____

_____

PART FOUR: LEARNING TO RISE

People have to learn process about everything. There should be no rush about jumping one step for another. People should have a grasp of timing and its importance to be able to rise and become resilient leaders. A great leader is one who builds a team of leaders but everyone in the team need to follow proper timing.

LESSONS TO BE NOTED
- Everyone is an emotional being and we need to understand that getting to rise is get up from our falls.
- Emotion is always driving when we are in a sullen or sad state.
- The state of reckoning is the stage where we know that we are emotionally hooked and curiosity is setting in.
- Not many people leave the process of reckoning. Very few people make it through reckoning because they allow the emotions to take the wheel and steer them to ground zero.
- People fight some self-worth and inferiority complex situations even when they are in the best team.
- Pain is hard. Ego doesn't own stories or love to write new endings. Ego likes blaming and hates curiosity. Pushing away all these emotions restores us to the path of healing from the fall.
- Hurt is not meant to be stockpiled. Emotions are undeniable.
- See realities and rise from the ashes of what has happened. A daring leader is one who leverages on fear to bring team members to be more courageous.

QUESTIONS

1. What can I do to understand when team members are hurt?

_____
_____
_____
_____

_____

_____

_____

2. How do I bring myself to understand other people's weakness and strength?

_____

_____

_____

_____

3. What more do I need to do to understand myself?

_____

_____

_____

_____

4. What are the other things for me to learn about myself?

_____

_____

_____

_____

_____

_____

_____

Made in the USA
San Bernardino, CA
30 July 2019